FUN FACT FILE: ANIMAL ADAPTATIONS

20 FUN FACTS ABOUT MARINE ANIMAL ADAPTATIONS

By Tayler Cole

Gareth Stevens PUBLISHING

Please visit our website, www.garethstevens.com. For a free color catalog of all our high-quality books, call toll free 1-800-542-2595 or fax 1-877-542-2596.

Library of Congress Cataloging-in-Publication Data

Cole, Tayler, author.
20 fun facts about marine animal adaptations / Tayler Cole.
pages cm. — (Fun facts file: Animal adaptations)
Includes bibliographical references and index.
ISBN 978-1-4824-4451-3 (pbk.)
ISBN 978-1-4824-4395-0 (6 pack)
ISBN 978-1-4824-4433-9 (library binding)
1. Marine animals—Juvenile literature. 2. Adaptation (Biology)—Juvenile literature. I. Title. II. Title: Twenty fun facts about marine animal adaptations.
QL122.2.C6524 2015
591.77—dc23

2015031498

First Edition

Published in 2017 by
Gareth Stevens Publishing
111 East 14th Street, Suite 349
New York, NY 10003

Designer: Andrea Davison-Bartolotta
Editor: Kristen Nelson

Photo credits: Cover, p. 1 Andaman/Shutterstock.com; p. 5 (octopus) Rich Carey/Shutterstock.com; p. 5 (shark) Shane Gross/Shutterstock.com; p. 5 (whale) Paul S. Wolf/Shutterstock.com; p. 5 (sea horse, cuttlefish) Kristina Vackova/Shutterstock.com; p. 5 (fish) Leonardo Gonzalez/Shutterstock.com; p. 6 Cigdem Sean Cooper/Shutterstock.com; p. 7 Raymond Connetta/Shutterstock.com; p. 8 Rachel Caauwe/Wikimedia Commons; p. 9 Citron/CC-BY-SA-3.0/Wikimedia Commons; p. 10 Peter David/The Image Bank/Getty Images; p. 11 Darlyne A. Murawski/National Geographic/Getty Images; p. 12 nicholas.voisin44/Shutterstock.com; p. 13 (top) Dorling Kindersley/Getty Images; p. 13 (bottom) Bill Curtsinger/National Geographic/Getty Images; p. 14 Jeff Rotman/Photolibrary/Getty Images; p. 15 (octopus) John Woodcock/Getty Images; p. 15 (background) Maria Zvonkova/Shutterstock.com; p. 16 Heather Lucia Snow/Shutterstock.com; p. 17 bluehand/Shutterstock.com; p. 18 Dimijian Greg/Science Source/Getty Images; p. 19 Vilainecrevette/Shutterstock.com; p. 20 © iStockphoto.com/Turnervisual; p. 21 Brian J. Skerry/National Geographic/Getty Images; p. 22 Dante Fenolio/Science Source/Getty Images; p. 23 Nina B/Shutterstock.com; p. 24 (top) Kjersti Joergensen/Shutterstock.com; p. 24 (bottom) Alexandra Lande/Shutterstock.com; p. 25 The Asahi Shimbun via Getty Images; p. 26 Yiming Chen/Moment/Getty Images; p. 27 BlueRingMedia/Shutterstock.com; p. 28 Chalermsak/Shutterstock.com; p. 29 Mint Images - Frans Lanting/Getty Images.

Printed in the United States of America

CPSIA compliance information: Batch #CS16GS: For further information contact Gareth Stevens, New York, New York at 1-800-542-2595.

Contents

Words in the glossary appear in **bold** type the first time they are used in the text.

Majestic Marine Life

Oceans are huge bodies of water with many **environments**, including different levels of water **pressure** and light. Over thousands of years, marine—or sea—animals have had to change their body and habits in order to survive. These changes are called adaptations. Each animal's adaptations depend on where it lives in the ocean.

Some marine animals have recently been discovered, like the blobfish. Others—such as whales—have been studied for hundreds of years. Get ready to learn about how many of them live deep underwater!

There are as many as 250,000 species, or kinds, of marine animals that have been discovered in the world's oceans. Scientists think there could be 750,000 more!

Fishy Adaptations

FACT 1

A puffer fish turns into a ball to keep predators away.

This sometimes spiky fish swims very slowly, making it seem easy to catch. In order to **protect** itself, the puffer fish takes in large amounts of water. Its body becomes a large ball predators can't fit into their mouth!

There's enough poison in one puffer fish to kill 30 people!

FACT 2

Puffer fish meat can be tasty—and deadly.

Parts of the puffer fish body are poisonous. In Japan, the nonpoisonous meat of a puffer fish is considered a treat. However, every year a few people are accidently poisoned after eating the wrong parts!

FACT 3

The blobfish has no bones.

The blobfish lives between 2,000 and 3,900 feet (610 and 1,190 m) deep in the ocean, where the water pressure is so strong it can smash bones! In order to survive, the blobfish has **developed** a body that's mostly a jellylike mass.

drawing of two blobfish

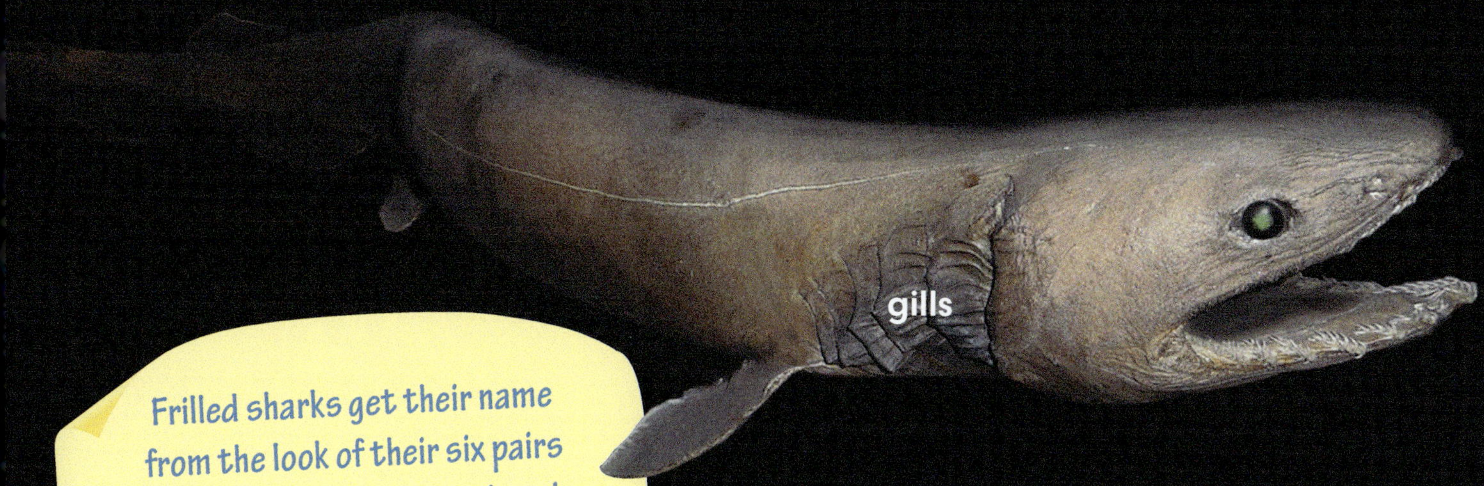

Frilled sharks get their name from the look of their six pairs of gills. Gills are the openings in a marine animal that allow it to breathe in water.

FACT 4

The frilled shark has about 300 teeth in 25 rows.

Living up to 5,000 feet (1,524 m) underwater, frilled sharks look like something from a horror movie! In fact, they often scare fishermen when found in shallow water. Frilled sharks use their terrifying teeth to catch squid.

FACT 5

The female anglerfish has her own built-in light!

The anglerfish lives so far below the ocean's surface that there's no light. So the female has developed her own light that hangs above her mouth. This light draws in other fish and brings them close enough for the anglerfish to eat!

FACT 6

A female anglerfish may have up to six males attached to her body.

Male anglerfish depend on females to catch food. A male uses his sharp teeth to attach to a female. Over time, he'll lose his eyes and other body parts from lack of use!

Beneath this female anglerfish, you can see a tiny male that's connected his body to the female's.

Shark Bite

FACT 7

Some sharks can put a new tooth in place of a lost tooth in just one day.

Sharks are continuously growing new teeth and losing old ones. The kind of teeth a shark has tell us what kind of food it likes to eat. Those that eat fish and larger animals have big, sharp teeth. Sharks that eat crabs and other shellfish have flatter teeth.

hammerhead shark

cookiecutter sharks feeding on a dolphin

FACT 8

The cookiecutter shark glows green.

The cookiecutter shark is bioluminescent, which means it makes its own light! The entire underbody of the shark is covered in tiny light-producing **organs**. These give off a green glow! Scientists think this helps to draw in **prey**.

The cookiecutter shark got its name because its perfect round bite mark is shaped a bit like a cookie cutter!

Amazing and Odd

FACT 9

Octopuses are master distractors.

When in danger, an octopus may let one of its eight arms separate from its body. The wiggling arm can cause a lot of confusion! The octopus may produce a cloud of black ink, too! These distractions give the octopus time to swim away.

Inside an Octopus

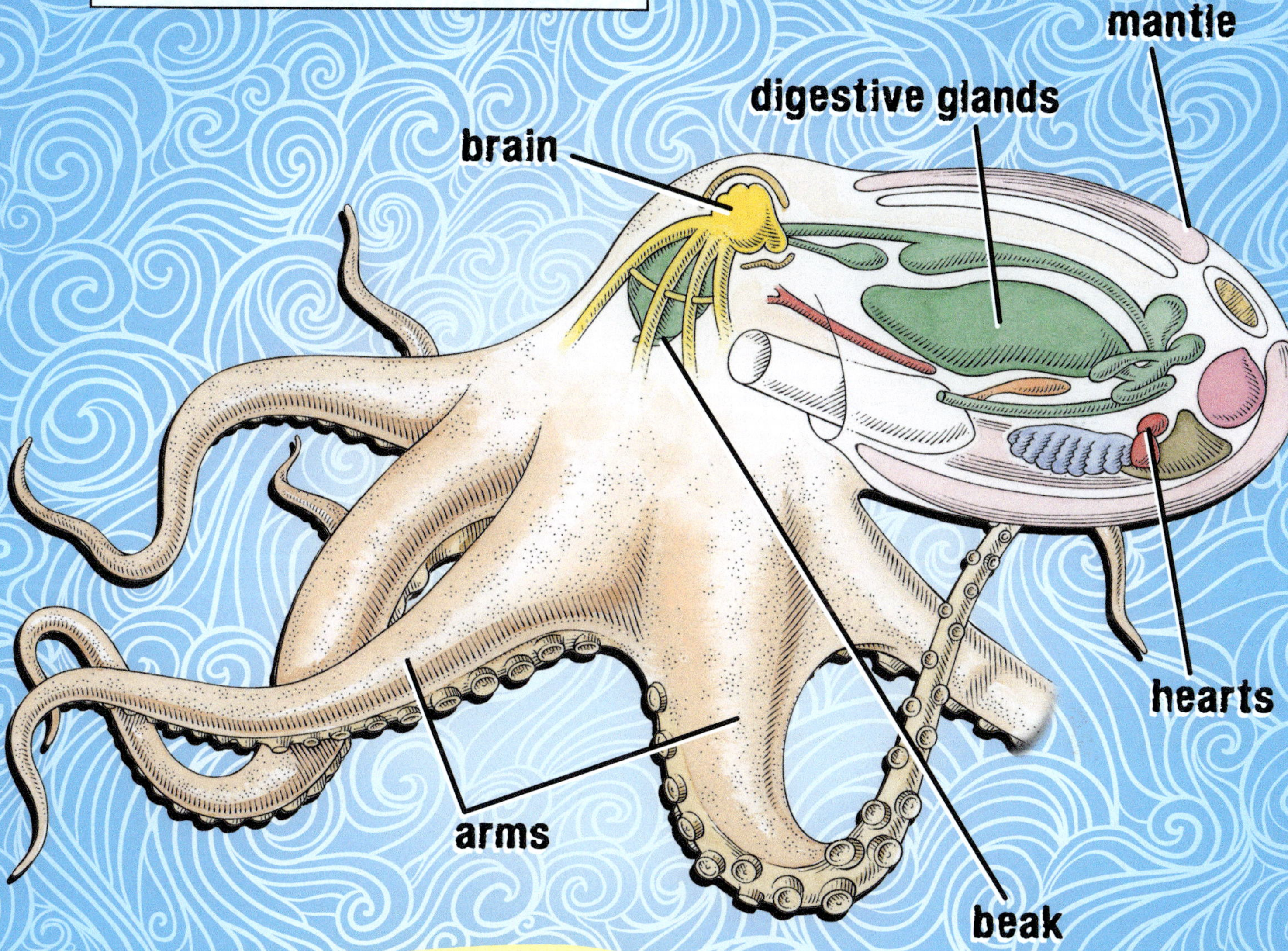

Octopuses have a lot of the same organs people do, such as a brain. But their organs are found in a big, headlike body part called the mantle.

Sea hares are a kind of sea slug.

FACT 10

Sea hares can be both mother and father at the same time.

Sea hares have **reproductive** parts of both males and females. One sea hare can be a male to another sea hare while acting as a female for a third sea hare! Many join together in a chain to produce millions of eggs!

FACT 11

Sea horses can look backward and forward at the same time.

A sea horse's two eyes move separately. This allows them to keep a look out for predators on either side of them without moving and giving away their position to nearby fish.

Even though they don't look like it, sea horses are a kind of fish!

Here you can see the male sea horse's rounded stomach before he gives birth.

FACT 12

Male sea horses are among the only male animals on Earth to give birth!

A female sea horse places her eggs into the male's pouch, where they are **fertilized**. He carries them until they **hatch**. This adaptation allows the female to begin producing more eggs right away.

FACT 13

Some sea stars have a stomach that comes out of their mouth!

Sea stars have two stomachs. One of them can be pushed out of the mouth to break down food outside the body. Then, the stomach goes back inside! The breakdown of the food continues in the second stomach.

FACT 14

One sea star can turn into five sea stars!

Some sea stars can regrow arms. But their arms can regrow bodies, too! Sea stars' most important organs are in the center of their body. An arm can become a brand-new sea star if it's still attached to part of the center body.

Sea stars can have more than five arms. This one has 11!

FACT 15

The jeweled umbrella squid tries to look like sunlight.

The jeweled umbrella squid is covered with tiny organs called photophores that produce light. Special muscles, or the body parts that allow animals to move, can direct the light. The photophores can show different colors, too!

Firefly squids are also covered in photophores. Groups of these squids put on quite a light show!

FACT 16

Cock-eyed squids' eyes are different sizes!

Cock-eyed squids seem to have a normal-sized right eye and a left one that's twice as big. The smaller eye watches for predators coming from below while the left eye, which has better eyesight, looks for the shadows of prey above.

Jewel squids are in the cock-eyed squid animal group. They live about 1,650 feet (503 m) deep in the ocean!

Home Sweet Home

FACT 17

Mother sea turtles return to the beach where they were born to give birth.

Even after years of being away, mother turtles know how to get to and recognize their birth beach. This is called natal homing, and scientists still aren't sure how it happens!

Sea turtle eggs that are too hot or too cold won't hatch at all.

FACT 18

Baby sea turtles become male or female based on the temperature inside their nest.

Temperatures between 83°F and 85°F (28°C and 29°C) produce a mix of male and female turtles. If the temperature is below this range, the turtles will be males. If the temperature is above 85°F (29°C), they will be females.

Jumping Jellyfish!

FACT 19

Some jellyfish are so big they can tip over a boat!

Nomura's jellyfish can grow up to 440 pounds (200 kg)! It's one of the biggest jellyfish in the world and can be as wide as a grown man. In 2009, a fishing boat near China netted dozens of these huge jellyfish—and the boat tipped over!

A Nomura's jellyfish is as heavy as an adult male lion!

FACT 20

The immortal jellyfish never dies.

Most jellyfish go through the same life cycle, which ends in death. Not the immortal jellyfish! When lacking food or injured, it turns back into a polyp, the part of the jellyfish's life between larva and adult. Then, the jellyfish begins its life cycle all over again!

The immortal jellyfish is tiny. As an adult, it's only about 0.18 inch (4.5 mm) across.

The first stage of the jellyfish's life cycle is the planula larva. It floats along in the ocean until it attaches to a rock. It develops into a polyp. It may turn into what looks like a stack of saucers—the budding polyp. Each saucer will turn into an ephyra and then an adult jellyfish, or medusa.

The Life Cycle of a Jellyfish

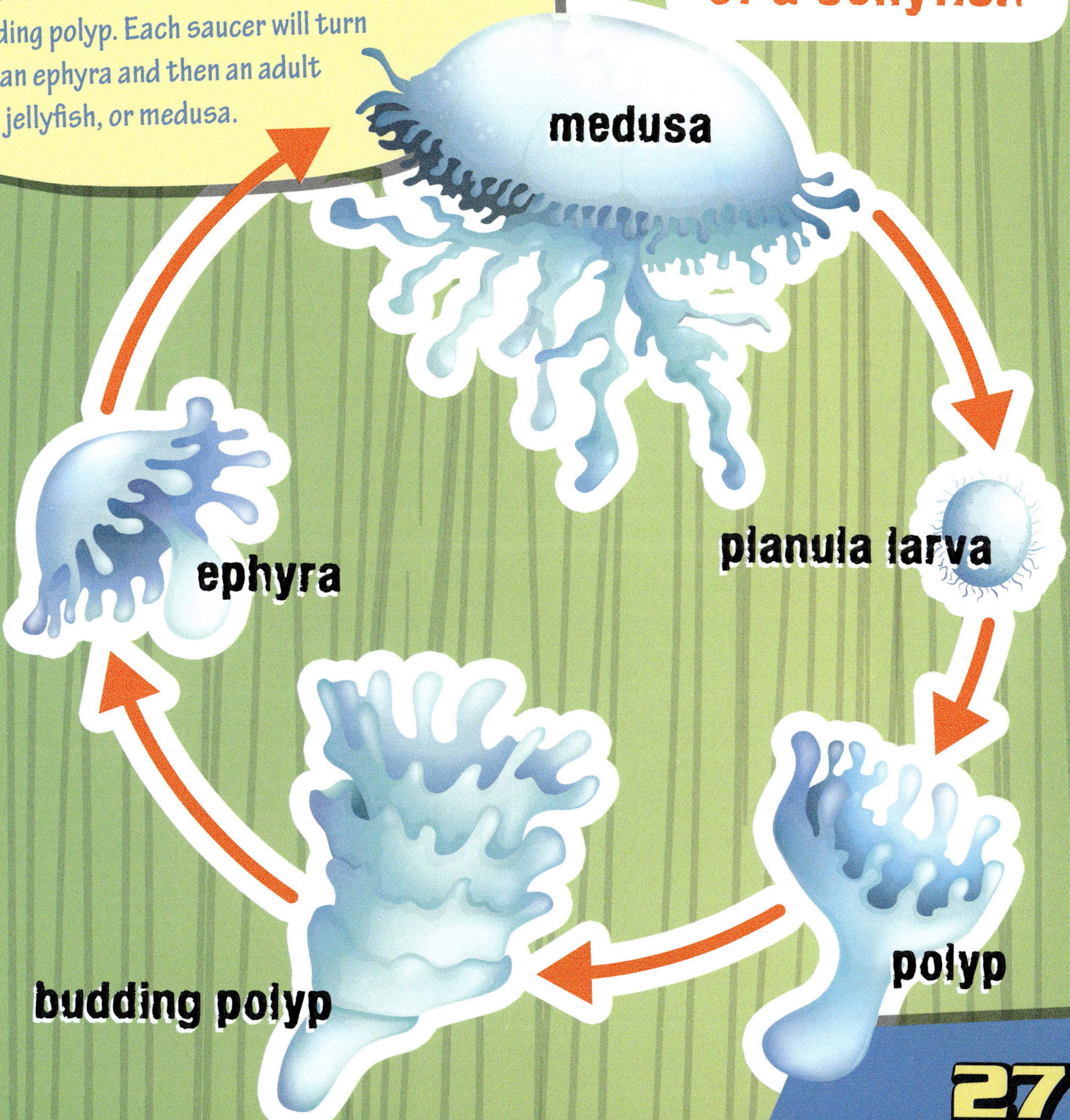

Adaptation Education

Almost three-quarters of Earth is covered in water. Under the surface live many types of marine creatures, such as the octopus, sea horse, and puffer fish. Without the special adaptations these species have developed, they would have died out long ago.

Scientists continue to study the amazing life deep in oceans and believe there's a lot more to learn about the animals that live there. If this interests you, aquariums, zoos, and natural history museums often have programs for kids who want to learn more!

Scientists who study life in the oceans are called marine biologists.

Glossary

attach: to fix to something

develop: to grow and change over time

distractor: one who distracts, or confuses

environment: the natural world in which a plant or animal lives

fertilize: to cause a new plant or animal to be created

hatch: to break open or come out of

organ: a part inside an animal's body

pressure: a force that pushes on something else

prey: an animal that is hunted by other animals for food

protect: to keep safe

reproductive: having to do with when an animal creates another creature just like itself

temperature: how hot or cold something is

For More Information

Books

Meister, Cari. *Totally Wacky Facts About Sea Animals.* North Mankato, MN: Capstone Press, 2016.

Owen, Ruth. *Anglerfish.* New York, NY: PowerKids Press, 2014.

Rizzo, Johnna. *Ocean Animals: Who's Who in the Deep Blue.* Washington, DC: National Geographic, 2016.

Websites

Octopus Facts for Kids
animalstime.com/octopus-facts-for-kids-amazing-facts-about-octopus-for-kids/
Learn more about how an octopus lives and reproduces. Be sure to check out the video at the end!

Ranger Rick: Seahorses
nwf.org/kids/ranger-rick/animals/fish/seahorses.aspx
Read more interesting facts about the sea horse, and look through amazing photos of the small bony fish!

Index